GETTING TO KNOW
THE U.S. PRESIDENTS

R O N A L D
REAGAN

FORTIETH PRESIDENT
1981 – 1989

WRITTEN AND ILLUSTRATED BY MIKE VENEZIA

CHILDREN'S PRESS
AN IMPRINT OF SCHOLASTIC INC.
NEW YORK   TORONTO   LONDON   AUCKLAND   SYDNEY
MEXICO CITY   NEW DELHI   HONG KONG
DANBURY, CONNECTICUT

Reading Consultant: Nanci R. Vargus, Ed.D., Assistant Professor, School of Education, University of Indianapolis

Historical Consultant: Marc J. Selverstone, Ph.D., Assistant Professor, Miller Center of Public Affairs, University of Virginia

Photographs © 2008: AP/Wide World Photos: 4 (Mohammad Sayad), 14, 15 top, 21; Corbis Images: 12, 15 bottom (Bettmann), 13 (Steven Clevenger), 23 (David J. & Janice L. Frent Collection), 24 (Bill Fritz-Patrick/White House/Sygma), 26 (Hulton-Deutsch Collection) 5, 30 (Peter Turnley), 3 (White House/Sygma), 17; Library of Congress/Paul Conrad: 25; Courtesy of the Ronald Reagan Presidential Library: 8, 10, 16, 18, 19, 29, 32.

Colorist for illustrations: Andrew Day

Library of Congress Cataloging-in-Publication Data

Venezia, Mike.
    Ronald Reagan / written and illustrated by Mike Venezia.
        p. cm. — (Getting to know the U.S. presidents)
    ISBN-13: 978-0-516-22644-6 (lib. bdg.)   978-0-516-26720-3 (pbk.)
    ISBN-10: 0-516-22644-4 (lib. bdg.)   0-516-26720-5 (pbk.)
    1. Reagan, Ronald—Juvenile literature. 2. Presidents—United
States—Biography—Juvenile literature. I. Title.
    E877.V46 2008
    973.927092—dc22
    [B]
                                        2006102976

President Ronald Reagan in the gardens of the White House in 1984

Ronald Reagan, the fortieth president of the United States, was born on February 6, 1911, in Tampico, Illinois. Before he became president, Ronald Reagan was a movie actor and TV star. He was also the oldest American president. President Reagan was seventy-seven years old when he left office.

An anti-American demonstration in Tehran, Iran, in the late 1970s

When Ronald Reagan became president in 1981, all kinds of frightening events were happening around the world. In the Middle East, Islamic militants were holding U.S. citizens hostage. There was lots of political unrest in nearby Central American countries.

The Soviet Union was building up its supply of deadly nuclear missiles aimed at the United States and its allies in Europe.

A 1980s military parade in Moscow's Red Square shows off Soviet missiles.

At home in the United States, there was a serious money problem called a recession. Many workers were out of jobs, and prices on almost everything kept going up. If things weren't bad enough, only two months after President Reagan started his job, he was shot by a crazed gunman named John Hinckley. Ronald Reagan soon recovered and got back to work. His confidence, sunny mood, and good sense of humor were comforting to people. They began to feel that President Reagan was a leader who might be able to solve any problem that came along.

Ronald Reagan as a lifeguard in Illinois at age sixteen

Ronald Reagan had an upbeat outlook on life from the very beginning. Even though the Reagans were poor, Ronald said he never knew it. Ronald's father was a shoe salesman. He kept moving his family to different locations, looking for the best sales jobs. As kids, Ronald and his brother Neil enjoyed exploring areas around the many towns and cities their family moved to.

The Reagans finally settled in the small town of Dixon, Illinois. Ronald made lots of friends in Dixon. During high school and college, Ronald worked as a lifeguard at a local park that was right on the Rock River. Ronald was proud to have saved as many as seventy-seven swimmers! He loved the attention he got, especially from local girls.

Ronald Reagan (right) as a baby with his older brother Neil

Ronald Reagan was never crazy about his first name. To sound more manly, he insisted that people call him by his family nickname, Dutch. When Ronald was born, his father said he looked like a "fat little Dutchman," and the name stuck.

Ronald did OK in school and enjoyed playing sports. He probably could have done better if his eyesight hadn't been so poor. Ronald never realized how nearsighted he was until he was thirteen. One day, for fun, he tried on his mother's eyeglasses, and was able to see clearly for the first time! Ronald was amazed by the way things really looked.

Reagan worked as a radio announcer in Iowa before becoming a movie actor.

As a teenager, Dutch Reagan really loved acting. He played parts in school plays whenever he got the chance. When he graduated from Eureka College in 1932, Dutch made up his mind to follow his dream. Dutch knew it was almost impossible to just go to Hollywood and become a movie star. So he tried the next best thing, which was to be a radio sports announcer.

Before people had TVs, radio was the main form of entertainment in the United States. Dutch landed a job at a small radio station in Iowa. He became well known as a baseball announcer. Then, while Ronald was on a trip to California, a friend arranged a screen test, or film audition, for him. A few days after returning to Iowa, Ronald received a contract from Warner Brothers Studio to act in movies!

Ronald Reagan and Jane Wyman in a scene from the 1940 film *Brother Rat and a Baby*.

As soon as his contract was signed, Ronald moved to California. He starred in movies and became very popular. Ronald loved making movies and meeting famous actors. In 1940, he married a beautiful movie star named Jane Wyman. A year later, when the United States entered World War II, Ronald was assigned to a special Army film division.

Ronald Reagan helped make training films for bomber pilots. When the war ended, Ronald was anxious to get back to his acting career. Things didn't go well, though. Ronald didn't get many good parts. In a movie called *Bedtime for Bonzo*, Ron had to share the spotlight with a chimpanzee!

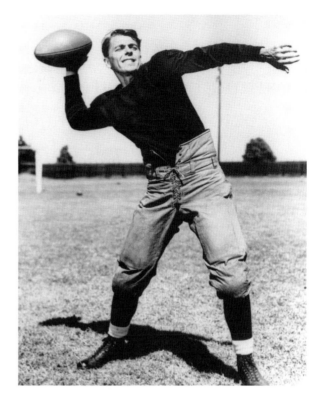

As an actor, Reagan is probably best remembered for his role as George Gipp in the 1940 film *Knute Rockne All American*.

Ronald Reagan and Diana Lynn in a scene from *Bedtime for Bonzo*

Ronald Reagan spent a lot of his time trying to find better parts. He also became involved in the actor's union, called the Screen Actor's Guild, or SAG. SAG helped actors get fair contracts with big movie studios. Ronald spent so much time working that he and Jane Wyman began to grow apart. Finally, their marriage ended in divorce.

Ronald and Nancy Reagan cut their wedding cake on March 4, 1952.

In 1947, Ronald was elected president of the Screen Actor's Guild. A short time later, he met another young actress, Nancy Davis. Ron and Nancy hit it off right away, and got married in 1952. Nancy was happy to give up acting and dedicate her life to Ronald and his career. Before she got out of the acting business, however, Nancy starred in a movie with Ronald.

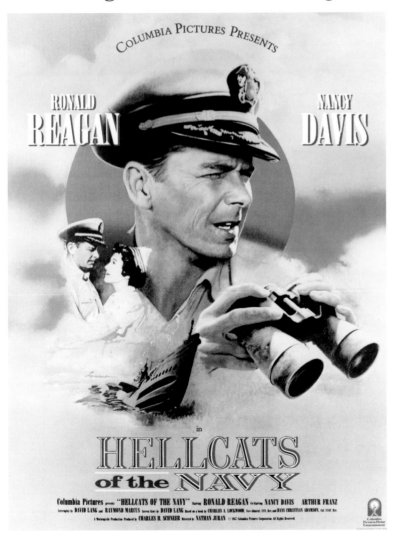

COLUMBIA PICTURES PRESENTS

RONALD REAGAN

NANCY DAVIS

in

HELLCATS
of the NAVY

Columbia Pictures presents "HELLCATS OF THE NAVY" starring RONALD REAGAN co-starring NANCY DAVIS · ARTHUR FRANZ

Before Nancy Reagan gave up her acting career, she starred with her husband in the movie *Hellcats of the Navy*.

Ronald and Nancy relax at home in California with their two children, Ron Jr. (left) and Patti (right). Reagan also had two children from his marriage to Jane Wyman.

Even though Ronald Reagan was very happy married to Nancy, his movie career was still in a rut. Then something happened that changed everything. Ronald was hired to be the host of a new television show, *General Electric Theater*. It was a great job.

Reagan as the host of the television program *General Electric Theater*

Ronald introduced a different television play every week, and became a spokesman for General Electric. He traveled around the country, giving rousing speeches to thousands of G.E. workers. General Electric was, and still is, a huge company that makes everything from electric toasters to rocket-engine parts. Ronald kept workers' spirits high by reminding them how their company was helping to make the United States such a great country.

In 1962, Ronald Reagan, who had always
been a Democrat, decided to join the Republican
Party. He and other Republicans believed the
federal government had grown too big, was
wasting money, and was taxing people way too
much. Ronald also felt the government was
putting too many restrictions on big businesses
like General Electric Company.

Ronald made his political feelings clear in the speeches he gave to G.E. employees. He also talked about his beliefs when supporting Republican candidates running for office. By 1966, leaders of the Republican Party were so impressed with Ronald Reagan they asked him to run for governor of California.

Reagan campaigns for governor of California in 1966.

Ronald Reagan won the election. Many people across the country couldn't believe a movie actor had become governor of California. Reagan's acting career had helped him a lot, though. He had a great look and speaking voice. People often felt like he was talking directly to them, even from the TV or radio. Ronald felt that traveling around the country meeting with G.E. workers had given him a good idea of what ordinary, everyday people wanted from their government.

Ronald Reagan served as governor of California for eight years. It didn't take Ronald long before he decided he might make a good president, too. In 1980, Ronald Reagan ran for president of the United States and won.

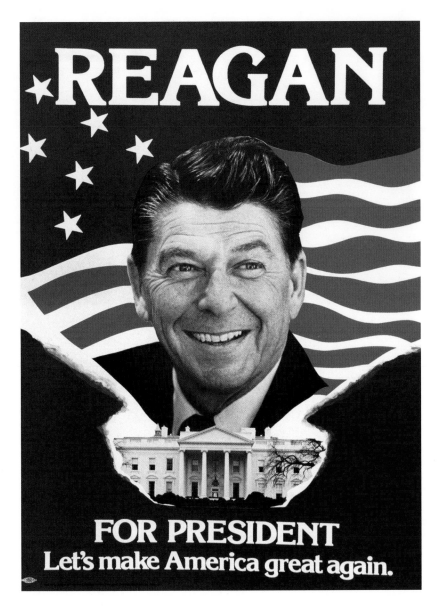

A 1980 Reagan presidential campaign poster

President Reagan salutes during a White House ceremony.

Ronald Reagan was ready to tackle the nation's problems. He had a plan for reducing the size of the government by cutting out some welfare programs and other services he felt were wasteful. He lowered taxes and built up the armed forces. Some of President Reagan's plans worked well, but some didn't.

President Reagan was criticized for spending tons of money on defense. Because of this, there wasn't very much left to help improve the country's inner cities, libraries, schools, roads, bridges, and national parks that needed aid.

This political cartoon by Paul Conrad shows Ron and Nancy pulling away in a car. It criticizes the huge deficit spending by the federal government during the Reagan years.

President Reagan was definitely against a wasteful government and high taxes. What he hated more than anything, though, was Communism. Communism was a system of government favored by the Soviet Union. The Soviet Union was made up of Russia and a group of republics it controlled.

Russian tanks roll down a street in Budapest, Hungary, after the Soviets invaded Hungary in 1956.

The Soviet government owned or controlled all the land, businesses, and factories in its republics. It set strict rules for its people, too. Communism was totally the opposite of the United States' free enterprise system.

The Soviet Union had forced its way of rule on a number of smaller countries after World War II. The Soviet government said they wanted all countries to become Communist some day.

This attitude started a war of words and threats between the United States and the Soviet Union. It was called the Cold War, and it lasted for decades. President Reagan felt it was worth spending billions of dollars to build up the military in order to protect the United States.

President Reagan believed a powerful
military would force Soviet leaders to respect
and listen to the United States. The president
hoped to discuss peaceful solutions for the
many problems between the two nations. By
the 1980s, each country had built enough
atomic weapons to destroy each other and the
entire world.

Luckily, in 1985, a new Soviet leader, Mikhail Gorbachev, came into power. President Reagan got along better with Gorbachev than he had with any previous Soviet leader. Over the next few years, each man agreed to dismantle many of his country's nuclear arms and missiles. The 1987 nuclear arms agreement was one of Ronald Reagan's greatest successes.

President Reagan chats with Soviet leader Mikhail Gorbachev in Geneva, Switzerland, in 1985.

President Reagan did have some flops, though. One of the worst was a mess he got into that involved a plan to free American hostages being held by Middle Eastern terrorists. President Reagan approved a secret deal to sell missiles to the Middle Eastern country of Iran to help win the hostages' release.

American hostage David Jacobsen (center) is reunited with his family after being released from Lebanon in 1986. Jacobsen was one of the hostages President Reagan was trying to free when he approved the secret deal to sell arms to Iran.

The Reagan administration used money from the Iran arms deal to secretly fund rebel fighters (right) in Nicaragua.

Even though the president believed he was doing the right thing, his decision was totally against United States policy. Things got even worse when it was discovered some of the money made in the deal was used to pay for a war that had not been approved by Congress. The Reagan administration had secretly sent money to rebel forces in Nicaragua to fight the Communist government in that Central American country. When the plan was discovered, President Reagan was forced to go on television and admit his mistake. This event became known as the Iran-Contra scandal.

President Reagan on his white stallion at his ranch in California

President Reagan's tax cuts helped people keep more of their money to spend on new homes, cars, and other products. By the time he left office in 1989, the economy was doing pretty well. The United States had the strongest military in the world, too. Unfortunately, spending so much on the military left the country trillions of dollars in debt. Also, America's poorest people felt ignored during the Reagan years.

Despite his ups and downs, Ronald Reagan was an extremely popular president. Reagan retired to California, where he spent time writing books and working on his horse ranch. After a ten-year battle with Alzheimer's disease, Ronald Reagan died in 2004 at the age of ninety-three.